MAZAS

ETUDES SPÉCIALES

Opus 36, Book I

FOR VIOLIN

(IVAN GALAMIAN)

Published in 2019 by Allegro Editions

Etudes Spéciales for Violin
ISBN: 978-1-9748-9987-6 (paperback)

Cover design by Kaitlyn Whitaker

Cover image: "Music Sheet" by danielo courtesy of Shutterstock; "Violin Front View Isolated on White" by AGCuesta courtesy of Shutterstock

ALLEGRO EDITIONS

ETUDES SPÉCIALES

Opus 36, Book I

VIOLIN

Edited by IVAN GALAMIAN

JACQUES FEREOL MAZAS
(1782-1849)

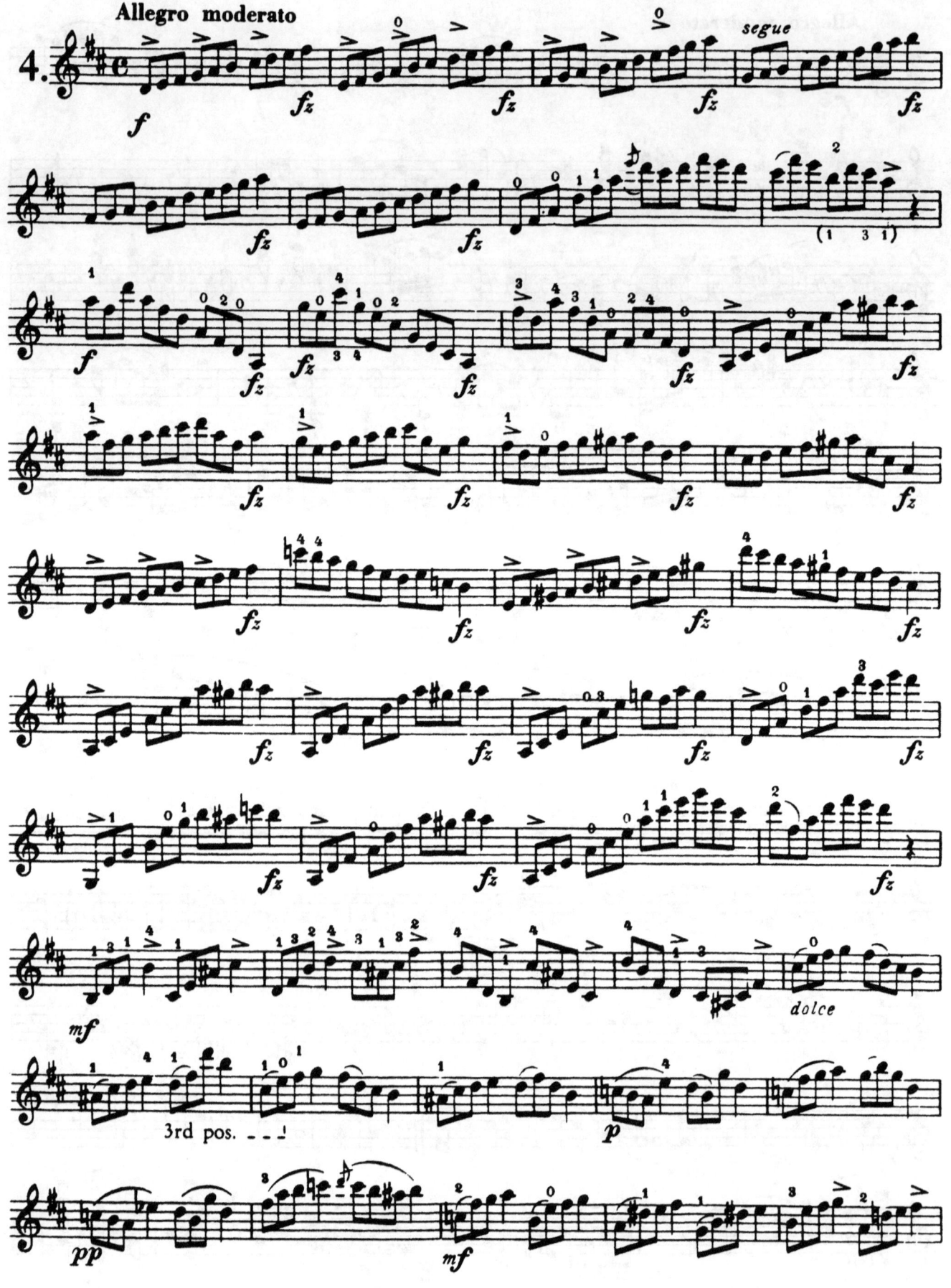

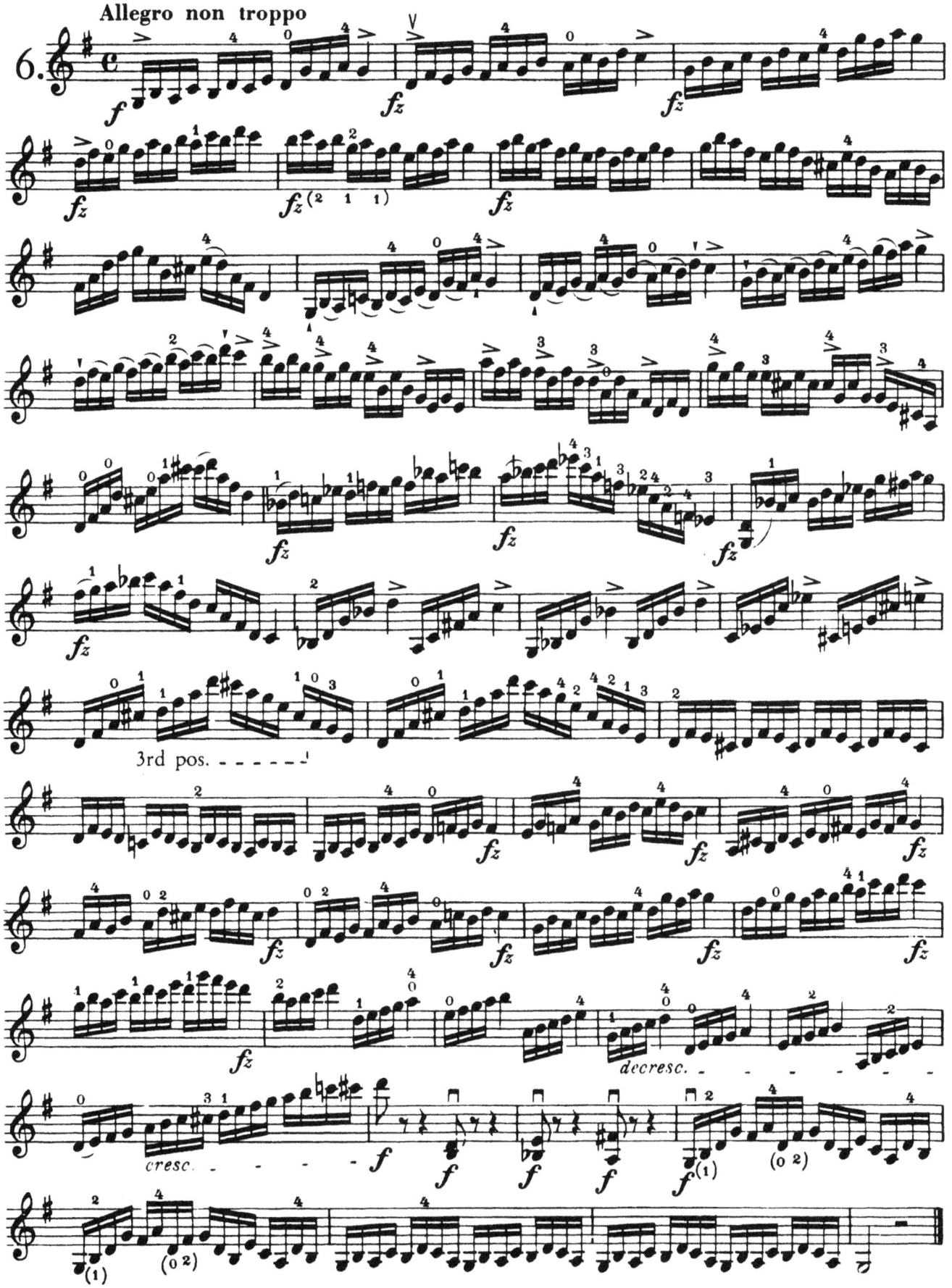

MARCHE
Allegro moderato

9.

Allegro

13.

17

ROMANCE
Andante grazioso

18.

24

Allegro

19.

25

27

Allegretto

21.

29

Allegretto quasi Andante

23.

31

dal Segno senza replica, sino al Fine.

POLONAISE
Allegro moderato

26.

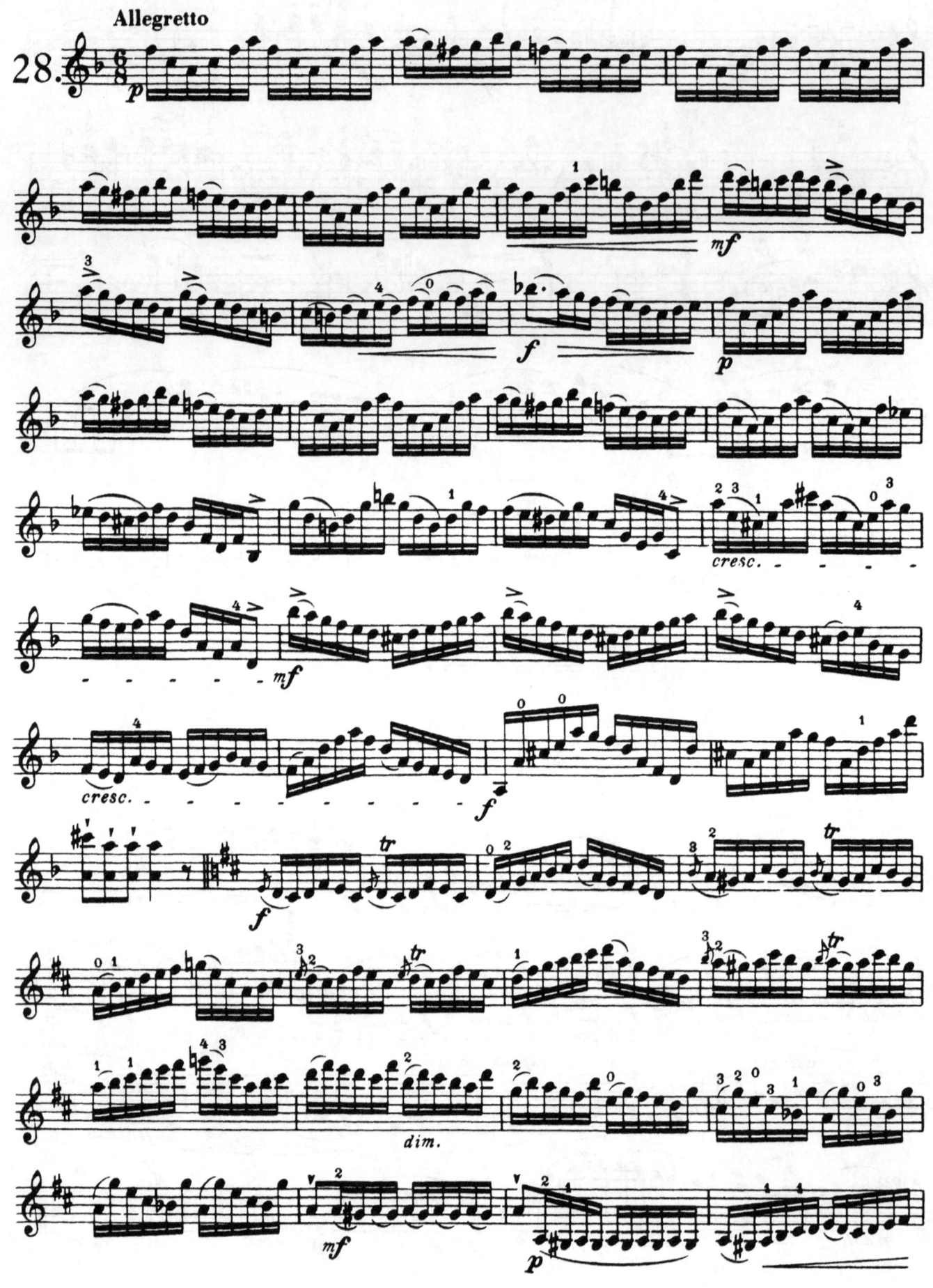

39

www.ingramcontent.com/pod-product-compliance
Lightning Source LLC
LaVergne TN
LVHW061344060426
835512LV00016B/2663